INSTANT ART
for the
CHURCH MAGAZINE

Book Four

Compiled and Illustrated
by
Roy Mitchell

Kevin
Mayhew

First published in 1994 in Great Britain by
KEVIN MAYHEW LTD
Rattlesden
Bury St Edmunds, Suffolk IP30 0SZ

Catalogue No 1396023
ISBN 0 86209 531 X

Cover by Roy Mitchell
Printed in Great Britain

Introduction

The demand for more 'instant art' has been so great that we are happy to satisfy the need with this, the fourth *Instant Art for the Church Magazine*. Roy Mitchell has produced a wide range of material covering a multitude of themes, and all with the needs of our regular users very much in mind. The 46 pages of high quality photocopiable artwork will be an asset to editors of a variety of church publications.

Flexibility/versatility

The book has been carefully designed to lie flat on the photocopier. Just select the size you require, cut out and stick the picture in place alongside your typed text.

Copyright

The material in this book is copyright-free, *provided that* it is used for the purpose for which it is intended. The usual copyright restrictions apply to any use for *commercial* purposes.

Readers' Responses

The 'instant art' series has been developing in response to ideas and suggestions from people who have used earlier titles. We would welcome any comments you might wish to make on existing books, and ideas for additions to the list are always carefully considered.

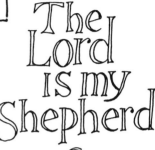

God fulfilled His promise at Easter

REJOICE! JESUS IS ALIVE!

A NEW LIFE IN JESUS

Celebrate the RISEN LORD!

HAPPY EASTER

JESUS IS ALIVE!

God so Loved the world that he gave his only Son...

Sunday

Monday

Tuesday

Wednesday

Thursday

Friday

Saturday

thought for the

Don't pray for a lighter load – pray for a stronger back...

thought for the

A CLEAR CONSCIENCE IS OFTEN THE RESULT OF A POOR MEMORY...

[INSERT 'DAY', 'WEEK' OR 'MONTH' AS APPROPRIATE]

THOUGHT FOR THE

The trouble with temptation is that it often comes gift-wrapped...

Thought for the

When a man is wrapped up in himself, he's over-dressed!

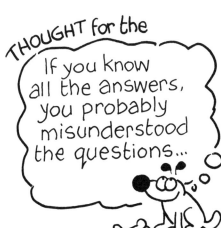

THOUGHT for the

If you know all the answers, you probably misunderstood the questions...

Thought for the

If you can find no fault in yourself, you need a second opinion...

JESUS SAID...

'...I AM THE RESURRECTION AND THE LIFE. HE WHO BELIEVES IN ME WILL LIVE, EVEN THOUGH HE DIES'

JOHN 11:25

JESUS SAID...

'...I AM THE LIGHT OF THE WORLD—WHOEVER FOLLOWS ME WILL NEVER WALK IN DARKNESS, BUT WILL HAVE THE LIGHT OF LIFE'

JOHN 8·12

JESUS SAID...

'...YOU CANNOT SERVE BOTH GOD AND MONEY'

LUKE 16·13

JESUS SAID...

'...NOTHING OUTSIDE A MAN CAN MAKE HIM UNCLEAN BY GOING INTO HIM— RATHER, IT IS WHAT COMES OUT OF A MAN THAT MAKES HIM UNCLEAN'

MARK 7·15

JESUS SAID...

'...WHERE YOUR TREASURE IS, THERE YOUR HEART WILL BE ALSO'

MATTHEW 6·21

JESUS SAID...

'...COME TO ME, ALL YOU WHO ARE WEARY AND BURDENED, AND I WILL GIVE YOU REST'

MATTHEW 11·28

JESUS SAID...

'... WHOEVER COMES TO ME I WILL NEVER DRIVE AWAY'

JOHN 6·37

JESUS SAID...

'...I TELL YOU THE TRUTH, ANYONE WHO WILL NOT RECEIVE THE KINGDOM OF GOD LIKE A LITTLE CHILD WILL NEVER ENTER IT'

LUKE 18·17

JESUS SAID...

WORRY WORRY WORRY WORRY...

'... DO NOT WORRY ABOUT TOMORROW, FOR TOMORROW WILL WORRY ABOUT ITSELF'

MATTHEW 6:34

JESUS SAID...

'... WHEN YOU STAND IN PRAYER, IF YOU HOLD ANYTHING AGAINST ANYONE, FORGIVE HIM'

MARK 11·25

JESUS SAID...

'...LOVE YOUR ENEMIES'

MATTHEW 5:44

JESUS SAID...

'...IF YOU HOLD TO MY TEACHING, YOU ARE REALLY MY DISCIPLES'

JOHN 8·31

From the Psalms

Cast your cares on the LORD...

...and he will sustain you...

Ps 55·22

From the Psalms

The LORD is compassionate and gracious...

...slow to anger, and abounding in LOVE...

Ps 103·8

From the Psalms

Search me, O God, and know my heart...

...test me and know my anxious thoughts

Ps 139·23

From the Psalms

Set a guard over my mouth, Lord...

...keep watch over the door of my lips

Ps 141·3

From the Psalms

How can a young man keep his ways pure?

THIS WAY

–by living according to your word...

Ps. 119·9

From the Psalms

A man who has riches without understanding...

...is like the beasts that perish

Ps 49·20

FROM THE PSALMS – 2

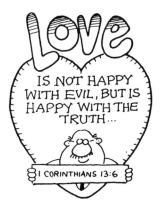

PILGRIMS...

GOOD SERMON TODAY...

THANK YOU...

...BUT IT WASN'T **ME**... IT WAS THE **LORD**...

IT WASN'T **THAT** GOOD...

PILGRIMS...

I'M KEEPING AWAY FROM CHURCH... IT'S **DANGEROUS**!

WHY?

MY GRANDAD WENT ON SUNDAY...

...AND HE SAID THERE WAS A **CANNON** IN THE PULPIT, THE CHOIR **MURDERED** AN ANTHEM, AND THE ORGANIST **DROWNED** THE CHOIR!

PILGRIMS...

WHO WAS THE PREACHER TODAY?

DUNNO...

WELL, WHAT DID HE PREACH ABOUT?

DUNNO— HE DIDN'T TELL US...

PILGRIMS...

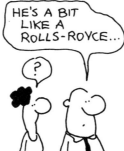

SO— WHAT DID YOU THINK OF THE PREACHER?

HE'S A BIT LIKE A ROLLS-ROYCE...

?

...INAUDIBLE, WELL-OILED, AND GOES ON FOR EVER...

TWINS! — CAN YOU SPOT THE TWO IDENTICAL SHEPHERDS?

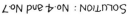

SOLUTION : No.4 and No.7

Use the letters which appear only once, to find the name of someone who appears in the Christmas story...

Use the letters which appear only once, to find the name of someone who spent some time in Egypt...

Snakes Alive!

Use the clues to fill in the circles on the snake. The last letter of each name is also the <u>FIRST</u> letter of the next one.

CLUES:

① He was captured and sent to Egypt.

② Samuel's mother.

③ He tried to have Jesus killed shortly after he was born.

④ He refused to stop praying to God, and was thrown into the Lions den.

⑤ His wife was turned into a pillar of salt.

⑥ He wouldn't believe that Jesus had risen from the dead.

⑦ Strong man of Israel.

BOOKMARK

Colour in the picture, then stick it onto a piece of card.

Cut it out carefully, to make a colourful bookmark.

Colour in the picture - Then stick it on a piece of stiff card. Cut around the dotted line, make a small hole at the top, and hang it up with a piece of thread.

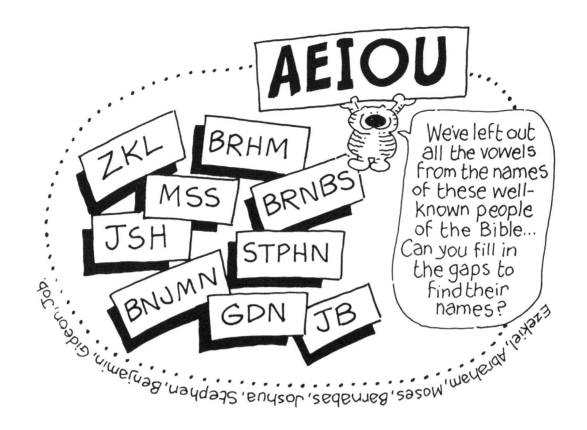

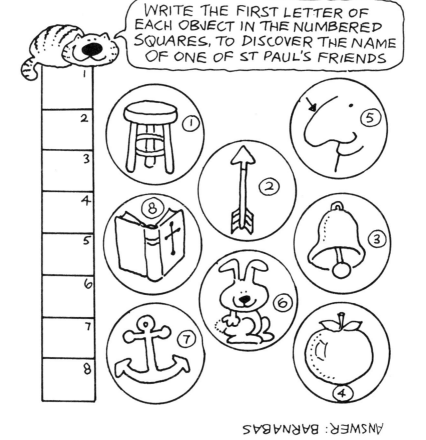

ANSWER: BARNABAS

CAN YOU READ THE LETTERS ON THE BRICKS TO FIND THE NAMES OF FIVE OLD TESTAMENT CHARACTERS?

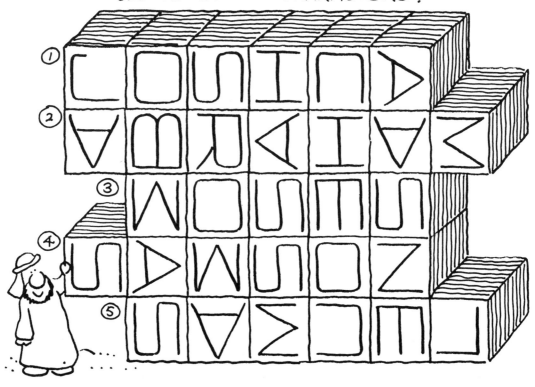

ANSWERS: JOSHUA, ABRAHAM, MOSES, SAMSON, SAMUEL